Cow Dung Theory
of Leadership

Published by Cow Dung Theory Company.

Title: Cow Dung Theory of Leadership:
A light-hearted look at serious career lessons

Author: Zoe Zi

ISBN 978-1-7348200-0-3

Ebook ISBN 978-1-7348200-1-0

Business | Leadership | Career

Book design by Venessa Lee. www.venessalee.com

Cartoons by Jonathan Brown. www.inkstains.com

First edition. 2020

Available at special discounts for bulk purchases.

info@cowdungtheory.com

www.cowdungtheory.com

Cow Dung Theory of Leadership

A light-hearted look at serious career lessons

Zoe Zi

Cow Dung Theory of Leadership

Table of Contents

Cow Dung Theory of Leadership

Foreword

I'm someone who has tried to move through life and not take myself too seriously, and try to call it like I see it. When you have that attitude, you look for kindred spirits. People who "get it". People who work hard, try hard and care, keep their sense of humour, and also have the insight to know when things are absurd or just plain wrong.

They have the courage to name those things. They call it out and identify a better way. They know real leadership when they see it. They support their people and push back to protect what is right. They don't sacrifice their values. They do what is right even when it affects what happens to them in a negative way.

Zoe is such a person. I had the privilege of working with her directly and indirectly over a number of years near the end of my 32-year run as a global management consultant, executive and business co-owner.

Cow Dung is a refreshing take on just a few of the things she experienced and dealt with over some of her career run. Zoe sees things that other people don't see and her humanity and judgment help her call it. And she can laugh at herself too. Zoe doesn't know all the answers and doesn't presume to; instead, you'll find that she invites you to consider the problem and opens your mind to possibilities that—it's true!—might require you to step into some piles of Cow Dung yourself.

Enjoy.

Paul Held
Executive Coach and Advisor
Retired Global Executive

Acknowledgements

SC gave feedback on all iterations of drafts, challenging me to make each story memorable and digestible in three minutes or less. VL brainstormed and tweaked illustration concepts with me. PH encouraged me to put the vignettes to good use.   Without their encouragement, *Cow Dung Theory of Leadership* would not be in print.

To my many mentors, especially MS, PH, RD and TE. Without their guidance, my professional life would not be one-tenth as fulfilling.

To Mom, Dad, Brother, Sister-in-Law, Niece (A), Niece (J), and Nephew.   Without them, I would not be who I am.

Z. Prologue

If someone made these predictions on the day I graduated, I would have said she was out of her mind:

- You will work for seven different companies, crossing two continents

- Your jobs will take you to over 30 countries

- You will survive two companies that filed for Chapter 11 bankruptcy

- In the first 15 years you will switch employers on average every 2.5 years. The next 15 years, you will stay at one company

- You will be a senior leader in a multi-billion-dollar company

- You will hold roles in sales, marketing, product management, private equity, consulting, financial management, strategy, technology, organization design

In 2019, the movie *Avengers: Endgame* was released. I binge-watched 12 movies in two weeks in order to get ready for the big event. Suffice it to say that I was infatuated with the Infinity Stones! I wrote these with me in mind. If I had possessed the Time Stone from the Marvel Cinematic Universe, I would go back in time to make sure I paid attention to these moments. These moments challenged my then-view of the known, and prodded me to push the boundaries and limitations of my mental model. Over time, they became some of the most pivotal lessons in my professional life.

You will meet me, my alter ego, my friends and colleagues. These are all real events. Names and organizations disguised to protect identities. Each of the five moments has a different theme: you, your team, your influence, your career, and then full circle back to you.

I take my work very seriously, but I don't take myself seriously. I hope you get a laugh out of these.

Leave me your thoughts at
www.cowdungtheory.com

A.
Why Are You Second-Guessing Me?!

Setting

I am on a high-profile strategic planning project. I lead one of three subgroups. All three subgroups are working under an executive with an important title.

Cast

In order of appearance; names modified to protect identities

Me: no introduction needed

Harry: executive with accolades galore, published articles on Harvard Business Review, etc.

Ricardo: my peer, leading another subgroup

Act 1.
Conference call. Ricardo and me in the same office. Harry on the phone.

> **Me:** Harry, can we talk about the model that you want Lisa to do?
>
> **Harry:** What about it?
>
> **Me:** Not sure we need a complex model to get the answer.
>
> **Harry:** It is a rather simple request. I want her to model the speed at which we will recover the initial investment, depending on how many units we fund.
>
> **Me:** I understand. Based on that, the answer is [this]. Unless you want to introduce another factor or vary the parameter, we won't need to do a model.
>
> **Harry:** [Reiterates his original request]
>
> **Me:** [Trying different ways to say no modeling is needed]

This goes on for a few rounds. Harry is sounding increasingly agitated. I'm banging my head on the table (silently). Ricardo is waving hand signals and mouthing the words: "LET IT DROP." Finally, it came to a head. Harry is yelling.

Harry: *[Saying my name syllable by syllable in crescendo],* why are you second-guessing me?!

What do you think happened next?

Act 2.

Ricardo: *[Hits mute on phone.]* Just please stop arguing with him. Let's get an intern to do this and take it off Lisa's plate.

Ricardo: *[Unmutes phone. In the calmest tone.]* Harry, we'll give it a go. How about we come back to this in a week?

Harry: Fine! *[You can hear the fury seething between his teeth.]*

In an alternate universe, my hands are reaching through the phone lines to strangle Harry by his throat.

Epilogue

I'm glad to report nobody got hurt and nobody got fired. I learned two things, one that day, and one a couple weeks later. The moment Harry said, "Why are you second-guessing me", something shifted. He pulled rank on me. He just confirmed that I was right and he was wrong. Growing up in the Asian education system, respecting authority was banged into our not-so-sub-consciousness. Layer on an additional unconscious bias suffered by most women. On that day, I smashed those biases. I am always cordial and respectful to everyone; but I no longer assume that people "more experienced" necessarily know more than I do. That mental shift sets me free on a growth spurt in my career.

A couple weeks later, the "model" was completed by an intern; it turned out as I expected, a linear function where the x-intercept is the answer I had provided. That "model" was never used, and Harry never pursued further. The second important lesson is that not every fight is won through hand-to-hand combat or logical debates. Ricardo knew. I didn't.

End credits

The astute reader would have noticed that Ricardo pulled me off the ledge and diffused the situation. It is very important to have friends at work who have your back, and of course you should have theirs in return, always.

B.
Cow Dung Theory of Leadership—it's not what you think

Performance reviews: the most anticipated and dreaded event of the year. Will you get a raise, a bonus, a promotion? Let's be honest, that's what you care about. Thirty annual reviews later, I only remember one sentence from one review. I got the top performance rating, with one developmental comment: you need to accept varying quality of work from your team.

This took place mid-career when I had already proven myself a strong leader. In my book, top-notch quality is non-negotiable. Accept varying quality? How would that make me a better leader? That comment periodically popped into my mind. After much exploration of frameworks, observing team dynamics, my own experiments and successes—I have condensed everything into my Cow Dung Theory of Leadership.

A leader's role is to set the vision, chart the course, motivate people to get things done.

Take that hill. Capture that flag.

Adapt your path, block and tackle.

> Your team needs to adapt to the terrain and obstacles that come their way. Having that freedom to make decisions gives them their sense of accomplishment and ownership. Incidentally, this is the key to delegation.

What is that pile of brown stuff that Joe is speeding towards? Is it…. Cow dung or land mine?

> Cow dung—let them run with it. It might be messy, but they will clean up, live and learn. Land mine—intervention needed. Because they (and thus we all) will get hurt. This is leadership.

There you have it: Cow Dung Theory. Simple. South Park cartoonish. Let me illustrate.

Lian was leading the annual department priorities process. Three days before the deadline, she wanted to conduct more analysis, including a review of external factors. From experience, I knew there was not enough time. Moreover, the strategy had just been refreshed 12 months prior; there had not been significant external changes that would meaningfully impact our priorities. I counseled her to delay the review of external factors until the following year. She was adamant that she could do it. Taking initiative is a great attribute.

I didn't want to curb her enthusiasm, so I let her proceed, knowing full well that it would be three days of long hours, but the results would not be useful.

On the other front, Joe had finished the business analysis of two entities. Entity A and Entity B provided different offerings to the same customers. He summarized the recommendation as, "Entity A and Entity B should integrate operations, share support resources, streamline processes to save money."   While I agreed, the reality was both Entities had been extremely profitable for many years. Both leaders valued the independent flexibility to quickly respond to customer needs.   Had we started with that sentence, neither would have listened to the merits of Joe's proposal. I had to intervene. Adjusting to a more finessed approach: using language of "coordination" rather than "integration", followed by a plan with stages and checkpoints so both Entities would see benefits and could control the pace of integration.

Lian was running towards a pile of cow dung; other than a few late nights for her and her team, no harm done.   Joe was about to step on a land mine; he would be kicked out of the room before either of the leaders would read beyond the first paragraph.

Accepting varying quality is not the same as accepting poor work. It is allowing your team to do it well, in a way that they own their accomplishments and feel good about themselves. It is providing the platform and freedom for them to cultivate confidence in themselves, while being there when they need the safety net. Cow Dung Theory of Leadership is differentiating between what will derail the initiative versus a harmless detour to the end goal.

C.
The Matrix Decoded

"I wouldn't be able to do your job. Everyone has an opinion and no one agrees. I don't know how you manage to get anything done!" This was one of the best compliments I got from a senior partner at a top professional services firm.

I am known for my ability to successfully navigate our matrixed organization. I am frequently selected to lead new initiatives with no natural home—new models that require departments to work together in a different way, and cannot reside solely in one department. I really want to write on my resume that my signature strength is herding big cats.

Herding cats is an important skill, especially if you are not in a command-and-control environment, regardless of function or industry. In this age of knowledge economy, people are the assets. Success requires you to bring people together. How does one get anything done with no authority over the other departments? Let me share a story.

Manisha, a senior executive, was appointed to a newly created position to bring four business units together. These four business units on paper reported to Manisha, but in practice, they were quite autonomous. While the four business units had grown over different trajectories, they were now increasingly interlinked, and it had become confusing for our customers when four sales people visited them to pitch.

There were many complex operational issues to resolve, and then there was also the more visible need to synchronize the way we represented our services on marketing materials, pitch books, website.   Website should be easy, right?   Manisha and I went through many meetings with each department head.   You would think they wouldn't care how a website looked? Oh, no, these strong personalities all had different opinions.   Rounds and rounds of discussions later, I became quite distraught; there was no way to arrive at a sensible option without pissing someone off. And I said as much to Manisha.

She responded, "*[Grasshopper, you have much to learn.]* As long as I have talked to every important stakeholder, I don't really care how the website looks."   Huh?! And I was sweating about how to elegantly incorporate everyone's conflicting feedback?!

Of course, Manisha said that with humor, and it was a coaching moment.   What she was doing was more sophisticated.   The discussions were meant to expose ideas, align objectives, understand concerns and gather input.   The website was not the ultimate prize.   More important was the underlying intention behind bringing the businesses together.   The resulting operating model (not just the website) was a composite, embracing the most appropriate ideas. Because Manisha had made the effort to engage, each leader's voice had been heard and incorporated. And she could point to where each leader had made contributions to the new go-to-market approach.

Navigating a matrix environment boils down to three basics:

1. **Align motivation.** Everyone wants a voice to shape the vision and destination.

2. **Reward egos.** Ego is not a bad word. According to the Merriam-Webster dictionary, ego means "the self especially as contrasted with another self or the world"; synonyms of ego include self-esteem. Everyone needs to be able to point to (or feel) their contribution to the successful outcome.

3. **You don't need to win every time.**

The third point is the hardest, especially for type A's out there (a-hem). Over the years I have always kept my secret formula in mind: Being 100% right with zero support, you won't get anything off the ground. Being 80% right with 100% support, you can go much farther and faster. I always bring a vision and proposal to the table, but I never hesitate to modify based on contributions from others. The art of influence is in getting everyone moving in an agreed direction with commitment and enthusiasm. If you can check your own ego in the process, you will have a much better chance of succeeding.

Happy trails through the matrix!

D.
Rules of the Game

I worked 15 years at one of the largest professional services firms in the world, held four roles with increasing leadership responsibilities. I must have known the rules of the game well, right?

The Regional Managing Partner of Asia Pacific hired me into the firm. Not long after, he was appointed Global Chief Operating Officer. He offered me the opportunity to join him in the Global Office, moving to the United States, to lead a similar function. It turned out to be an exhilarating four years in the Big League. I was a top performer, led important work, with lots of visibility to global executive leadership.

An important rule of the game in the firm is every four years there is a Global CEO election, and with that a new leadership team chosen by the CEO-elect. I predicted that my boss would be re-appointed and my team would stay intact (I was right), that I would advance my career and have bigger impact, while continuing to work with someone who trusted me and someone I respected. I kicked into high gear: documented my team's accomplishments, mapped the vision for the coming four years; summarized a two-page document titled "Looking Back: Looking Forward"; secured an appointment with the Global COO, a-hem, feeling like a visionary leader myself.

This is how the meeting went:

[Boss reads the two-pager in under one minute.]

Boss: That is why I have been asking you over and over again what you want to do.

Me: *[Not quite registering... My inner voice: Isn't my four-year plan what I want to do?]*

Boss: It is a bit late now, the Executive Team design is set.

Me: *[Huh? I still lead a team reporting to you. What do you mean?]*

Boss: *[Pulls up the new organization chart and turns the monitor over to show me.]* New leaders have all been appointed, and most have picked their teams. If you had come two months ago, I would have been in a better position to help you get an expanded or a different role.

Me: *[Deer in the headlights. I have not yet made a sound.]*

He then went through the entire organization chart. "Group A - you will need recent client service experience to be credible, so not a feasible choice. Group B - the leader will retire in four years, so perhaps be her right hand and aim for the leader role when she retires. Leader of Group C is new to global office, has not finished picking her team, so a possibility there. Group D is a new concept therefore a more risky bet. *[This continued group by group.*

In conclusion...] You should approach Jack and Jill. Explore a possible role in either team if you want to plan a growth path to the executive level."

I left his office shell-shocked. Then it clicked; I never paid attention to the tactics of HOW to play this game!

Fortunately my story ended well. Within one month, I landed on a dual-role assignment. I continued to lead my team under the Global COO, and in addition I was the Chief of Staff to the Global Executive Leader of all revenue-generating service lines. That set me on a trajectory for another eight great years. How I got my dual-role sorted out in the tight one-month timing is another story, for another time.

I wish I had known. The moment you land on a job or a promotion, in addition to delivering strong performance, you need to set your bearings ahead. Because all these prerequisites to a successful progression take time to congeal: demonstrating results in your current role; gaining knowledge about the target responsibilities; establishing relationships with people in target groups; putting yourself on the radar so leaders will think of you as a possible candidate when an opportunity arises. It is planting seeds and nurturing them to blossom. That's HOW the game is played.

E.
Happy Folder

My work inbox is insane. 16,347 messages and typically 500 to 800 unread. That's just the inbox. We have not counted the folders yet. Way back, I had a folder for each project. That required diligent filing, so when my responsibilities increased, the filing system fell apart. My calendar is packed back to back starting around 8am or 9am, with the last meeting ending at 7pm on a good day. Filing emails? Not a priority.

How do I find anything? It's in my head. I remember who sent me what, roughly when, and I use the search function, who needs folders? By the way, I don't recommend this method, that's not the point of this story.

There is one special folder. It's Happy Folder. Yes, that is the label: "Happy Folder". I don't remember where I got this idea, it probably morphed from one of those self-help book tips: track accomplishments to be ready for year-end performance review or updating your resume.

Happy Folder is as advertised. When an email puts a beaming smile on my face, and if it is a lucky moment when my brain is not obsessed with the next task (very seldom), I file a copy. On any average day, I don't remember what has been stored in it. On a tough, soul-crushing day, I take a peek.

Early 2019, I needed to turn in my work laptop. So I purged and archived. Some statistics on Happy Folder:

- 19 emails total, the first was from February 2016. Of which,

- 7 are people commending me on successful outcomes

- 6 are hilarious exchanges with friends, or unexpected humor from unexpected people

- 3 are proud moments: taking an unpopular stance on a topic; handing the reins of a program that I built from the ground up to a successor

- 2 are from my team saying the way I handled challenging situations inspired them

- 1 is a simple hello from a leader who answered my emergency call for advice

Happy Folder did not help keep my resume up to date. Yet, every email still puts a smile on my face. Surprisingly, it is most gratifying to read the two notes about the positive influence I left on my team, not the seven commendations of projects completed well. Re-living how I felt when that leader responded to my outreach for help, reminds me why I always say yes when someone needs to talk.

I cannot summarize the key takeaways for you. On the simplest level, Happy Folder carries you through the difficult days. There is more, however, if you are ready to look beyond. Happy Folder is a montage. There were no goals or categories when I started collecting. The montage takes shape when you dap color on the canvas, over time layering on more in one area than another. Clarity emerges when you step back to take it in. It is both a gift and a lesson, but ones that only you can give yourself.

Happy collecting. I wish I had started a whole lot earlier.

About the Author

Zoe Zi grew up in Asia, studied in North America, and moved back and forth a couple times between the two continents. While her career path may seem like a series of unplanned coincidences, things turned out pretty well for her, reaching the top leadership ranks of a big, big, big multi-billion dollar company. Along the way, Zoe met a lot of interesting people: some became mentors, many grew into long-lasting friendships. She feels very blessed in her life and hopes *Cow Dung* will entertain as well as inspire you, as her mentors and friends have done for her. By the way, Zoe Zi is a pen name; the author still has to pay rent, and presently earns a living advising type A executives, many of whom are very (too) serious.

More Cow Dung Theory

I hope you enjoyed the vignettes and got a few laughs out of them.

Cow Dung Theory of Leadership is available in print and e-book.

ISBN 978-1-7348200-0-3

Ebook ISBN 978-1-7348200-1-0

Available at special discounts for bulk purchases.

info@cowdungtheory.com

www.cowdungtheory.com